# Introduction

CW00531508

This series aims to heighten pupils' awareness of technological aspects of everyday objects, events and experiences that, in the absence of prompting, people tend to take for granted. It looks at familiar things in an unfamiliar way. As one teacher commented on first seeing Programme 6: 'Who would have thought that a postbox could be so interesting? I've never really considered one in that way before.'

All the programmes relate to children's experiences. Programmes 1 to 5 look at technology in and around the home. Programmes 6 to 10 go further afield – into the street, the playground, the park, and onto main roads – to places as diverse as a foundry, a football factory, a giant amusement park and a rubbish dump.

The series stimulates inquisitive minds. For pupils, there are insights into how things work and why they are as they are. For teachers, the first five programmes include school scenes showing children making use of follow-up ideas found either in this guide or in the accompanying activity book (see the inside back cover for details). The suggested tasks encourage pupils to show imagination and inventiveness, and to adopt the principles and practices of the sequence 'plan, design, make, test, review, evaluate'. The follow-up work can be as challenging as you, the teacher, care to make it.

Channel 4 Schools welcomes comments on its output. If you have any views on this series and any news of developments arising from the series that you would like Channel 4 Schools to know about, please write to me at the address given below.

Robert Wilson
Education Officer, Channel 4 Schools
Educational Television Company
PO Box 100
Warwick
CV34 6TZ

## CONTE

# About the series

## Using the programmes

The programmes constitute a series but they do not constitute a course. The sequence in which they are presented may not be the sequence in which you most want to use them. For example, your curriculum plan may start with a study of technological aspects of water, to which Programme 7 would make a useful contribution. There is no great loss in showing programmes out of sequence. This is particularly true of Programmes 6 to 10.

In order to show programmes in a way best suited to your needs, the programmes will probably have to be recorded. As part of its service to schools, ETC sells videotapes of this series. See the inside back cover for details.

A videotape of the series has other advantages. Given the scope that each programme offers for follow-up work, you may wish to wait more than a week before using another programme in the series. Also, each programme may be divided into several sections. A videotape allows you to show just the snippet you want pupils to see. For example, when using Programme 6 it is possible to choose to look at telephones but not at postboxes, which can be saved for another occasion.

## Classroom scenes

Classroom scenes are included in Programmes 1 to 5. They serve to give you and your pupils an idea of the types of activity that some 9 – 11 year olds are tackling, but they do not claim to show model lessons; you will spot imperfections in what takes place. Bear in mind that at this age and stage it is the approaches to learning which are vital; the quality of the final product is markedly less important than the quality of the learning process.

## Curricular links

The series is not tied to any particular curricular pattern, nor does its relevance and appeal depend on a particular and possibly transient policy towards the teaching of technology to primary school pupils.

### Programme main themes

| Title | Main theme | Context |
|---|---|---|
| Constructive Thoughts | Finding solutions to specific problems | Housebuilding |
| Safe and Warm | Designing, testing and using known technology | Electricity |
| Gadgets at Work | Functional design's contribution to people's welfare | Kitchen |
| Making for Success | The vital role of planning and organisation | A big party |
| Good Riddance | Environmental aspects of technological progress | Rubbish |
| Street Wise | The variable pace of technological change | Street furniture |
| Water Works | Technology's contribution to human welfare | Water supply and use |
| Safe Ways | Using technology to make roads safer | Roads and motorways |
| Park and Ride | Technology's contribution to having fun | Play and pleasure parks |
| On the Ball | Technology's contribution to ball games | Football and tennis |

# Curricular coverage of
# Living With Technology

This table indicates, in summary form, the main areas of a technology curriculum to which the series can make a worthwhile contribution. Each of the descriptions approximates to a feature in one or more of the technology curricular documents currently extant within the UK. The extent to which any one programme makes a contribution to the areas listed below depends only partly on the programme's content. It also depends on how a programme is used, on which follow-up activities are selected and on how much time is devoted to follow-up work.

## Knowledge and Understanding

### Understanding and using technology in society

- ▶ understand ways in which technology has met and meets human demands

- ▶ identify the impact of technology on industrial processes

- ▶ identify the impact of technology on lifestyles and the environment

- ▶ know ways in which technology enables an environment to be controlled

- ▶ understand some ways in which developments in technology and changes in social and aesthetic values determine design criteria

### Understanding the design process

- ▶ identify and state needs and opportunities for design

- ▶ understand the processes of designing and manufacturing

- ▶ relate design and function

- ▶ evaluate process and product against key criteria

## Skills and Techniques

### Using the design process

- ▶ collect evidence to identify need and function

- ▶ determine the function of something from its design

- ▶ fulfil a task by devising and carrying out a plan

- ▶ design, construct and test an artefact against design criteria

- ▶ use and make devices and tools associated with control mechanisms

- ▶ devise a fair test

- ▶ evaluate an artefact for effectiveness and efficiency in use

## Values and Attitudes

- ▶ recognise the impact of technology on society

- ▶ care about the impact of technology on the environment

- ▶ show interest in the scope of technology for enhancing quality of living

# Constructive Thoughts

## Learning outcomes

**The programme considers:**

- materials used in housebuilding
- structures used in housebuilding
- housebuilding techniques
- how to move heavy loads
- safety on building sites.

**After viewing the programme and undertaking the activities suggested, pupils should have made progress in:**

### Knowledge and Understanding

▶ understand how technology is used in building

   explain what makes structures strong

   describe how to move heavy loads

   explain how vital services (e.g. water, electricity, gas) are supplied to homes

   understand the need for safety at work.

### Skills and Techniques

▶ plan, design, build simple strong structures

   plan, design, build simple lifters and carriers

   evaluate the worth of a design

   use tools appropriately and safely.

### Attitudes and Values

▶ appreciate the role of planning and design in housebuilding

   empathise with owners of new homes.

## Programme synopsis

We see work on a housebuilding site, e.g. laying foundations and floors, waterproofing, making mortar, building walls. The dangers of building sites are stressed – children, keep out! Materials and techniques for 'building for strength' are shown and discussed. Potential problems, and their solutions, are seen, e.g. moving loads, building high walls.

Pupils are seen in a classroom using materials (e.g. paper, wood, plastic), tools and techniques to make strong structures, with emphasis on designs based on interlocking and on frames using triangles.

A safety rap urges safe practice. Back on site, heavy loads are seen being moved.

In the classroom, pupils simulate site activity and devise their own ways (some simple, some sophisticated) to move and lift loads by making use of frames, levers, wheels, cogs, pulleys and various materials.

Back on site, the McDonalds come to inspect progress on their incomplete house. We see provision made for connecting vital services, which await fitting and testing. This links back to the classroom, where strength tests are literally in full swing.

## Key vocabulary

site, materials, machines, foundations, joists, mortar, frog, staggered pattern, interlocked, scaffolding, structures, site agent, effective, efficient.

## Before the programme

▶ Find out what pupils already know about building and building sites, e.g. jobs done, materials, tools, machinery, techniques, dangers, safety precautions.

▶ Find out what they already know about the services connected to many homes.

▶ Stress the planning that goes into building a new housing estate, e.g. the site plan, allocation of land to different uses (houses, shops, parks).

▶ Stress the need to design houses before building them, and the need for accurate drawings for builders to follow.

▶ Inform pupils that the programme is about making houses strong, durable and safe.

▶ Inform them that they will be given a chance to plan, design, build and test strong structures.

**Note:**

The programme, which should be taped, can be viewed wholly or in part. Natural breaks occur where scenes switch from building site to classroom and vice versa.

# During the programme

Pupils should be asked to view the programme with one or more purposes in mind. Tasks may be allocated to individuals or to groups and could include identifying:

a materials used in building a house

b health and safety precautions on site

c ways of moving materials on site

d how house walls are made strong

e how essential services reach homes

f materials used by pupils on screen

g tools used by pupils on screen

h range of models made by pupils

i the messages of the safety rap.

# After the programme

? Which parts of the programme did you find easiest/hardest to understand?

What do you now understand better?

**Programme 1** emphasises solving problems linked to building technology, so give pupils tasks which set problems requiring them to make items capable of meeting specified needs/targets. Pupils' success depends on designing and building 'for strength' i.e. on the proper use of suitable materials.

Pupils can attempt the following:

1 Design, build and test walls of differing materials and structures to find out which combinations are the most successful in terms of strength, ease of construction, cost and aesthetic appeal.

2 Using straws, rolled paper or a technology kit; design, build and test a scaffolding to support a given load.

3 Design, build and test a structure (e.g. a frame) and a mechanism (e.g. a pulley system, a lever system) which will move a load of specified weight from ground level to a specified height.

4 Design, build and test a powered vehicle which will move a specified load a given distance in a given time.

Pupils' output can be evaluated in 3 ways:

## Effectiveness

The test: Can the artefact do what it has to do? Does it meet required performance specifications? Yes? No? Sometimes? (If sometimes, why only sometimes?) Is there any virtue in exceeding target performance?

## Efficiency

This test considers the cost of making the device effective. What resources has it used up (quantity) and at what cost? A vehicle which does the same job using fewer resources than its rival (by volume and/or by value) is superior to its rival.

## Aesthetic appeal

How does the thing look? Beautiful? Ugly?

In each case pupils should be encouraged to consider a number of ideas; to plan and design their construction; and to make, test and evaluate their product. Stress the need for careful planning and designing prior to attempting construction. Pupils should also be asked to present a final report which:

a gives details of materials and structures used

b provides evidence of testing the product for quality and effectiveness

c offers an evaluation of the worth of what they did (processes, procedures, product).

---

## RESOURCES

Bricks in a variety of materials, adhesives, plasticine, straws, pipecleaners, newspaper, a variety of papers, pulley wheels, cog wheels, technology kits, appropriate tools, a variety of working toy machines and/or kits to build them; a collection of materials used for building a real house.

# Safe and Warm

## Learning outcomes

**The programme considers:**

- electricity generation using hydro-power

- electricity supply networks

- using electricity in the home

- using electricity safely

- making simple circuits for various uses

- electrical conductors and insulators

- uses of switches within a circuit.

**After viewing the programme and undertaking the activities suggested, pupils should have made progress in:**

### Knowledge and Understanding

▶ understand how electricity is generated

understand how electricity is supplied

understand the nature of a circuit

understand the role of switches

know some uses of electricity in the home.

### Skills and Techniques

▶ be able to construct a simple circuit to light a lamp or work a buzzer

be able to test materials for their insulating/conducting properties

be able to construct a simple switch using insulating and conducting materials

be able to solve problems related to using a simple electricity circuit.

### Attitudes and Values

▶ be aware of the need for safety procedures when dealing with electricity

be aware of how electricity affects people's lives.

## Programme synopsis

The McDonalds' house is ready for them to move in. We see the service facilities that await them within it.

Mains electricity is vital to them. We see hydro-electric power being generated and being supplied through the grid system. In a school, pupils are making low-volt electricity work; circuits are devised, built and tested to illuminate bulbs and to sound buzzers.

The McDonalds move in and try out the electric fittings, particularly the switches. Back at school, pupils are discovering electrical conductors and insulators as a prelude to designing and making switches and putting them into circuits. The safety rap is repeated.

Back at the house, automatic safety switches are looked at. Finally, we see pupils testing burglar alarms for which they have designed circuits and made activating switches.

## Key vocabulary

electricity, plastic sleeves, mains, generator, energy, hydro-electricity, valve, turbine, pylons, battery, bulb, switch, conductor, insulator, terminals, circuit.

## Before the programme

▶ Tell pupils that the programme is largely about electricity and how we use it.

▶ Find out what they already know about electricity.

▶ Alert pupils to the dangers associated with high-voltage electricity.

▶ Convince them to use only low-volt batteries when investigating electricity.

▶ Let them handle some low-volt electrical items, e.g. torches, batteries, toys.

## During the programme

Pupils should be asked to view the programme with one or more of the purposes listed below in mind.

To find out:

1 how electricity is generated and supplied to homes

2 a number of uses for electricity in the home

3 safety procedures needed when using electricity.

# After the programme

**?** What did you gain from the programme?

Which bits need further explanation?

The emphasis of the programme is on designing and constructing circuits that incorporate switches. Pupils should use materials to construct simple circuits which have a variety of applications. The emphasis should be on designing, making and testing circuits, and the final products should be evaluated for their effectiveness and reliability. A core theme should be how to use electricity safely. Some activities should be done by all pupils to promote basic understanding. Other tasks can be group-related.

**1** All pupils should be asked to construct a simple circuit using a battery, wires and a bulb (see Helpful Hints, page 24). Crocodile clips are an optional extra.

**2** All pupils should incorporate a simple switch correctly within a circuit (see Helpful Hints).

**3** All pupils should test materials for use as electrical conductors/insulators.

**4** All pupils should be given the task of finding out safety procedures related to electricity. This task may take the form of a picture where pupils identify problem areas in, for example, a kitchen.

**5** Individuals or groups should carry out selective research tasks, e.g. on finding out how electricity is made, how it flows through a circuit and how fuses and other features of mains supply (e.g. cordless kettles) contribute to electrical safety.

**6** Individuals, pairs or groups should be given at least one of the following projects:

▶ Design, make and test a lighthouse.

▶ Design, make and test a burglar alarm using a lamp or a buzzer.

▶ Design, make and test a warning device for a vehicle.

▶ Design and build an electrically-motorised vehicle.

▶ Design and build a game using a simple circuit (see Helpful Hints).

## Extension activities

These will require pupils to do research on more complex electrical arrangements e.g. parallel circuits and two-way switches.

▶ Design and build a model house, incorporating a lighting system including bedside lamps, main room lights and a light using a two-way switch (e.g. hall light).

▶ Design a model street with a lighting system.

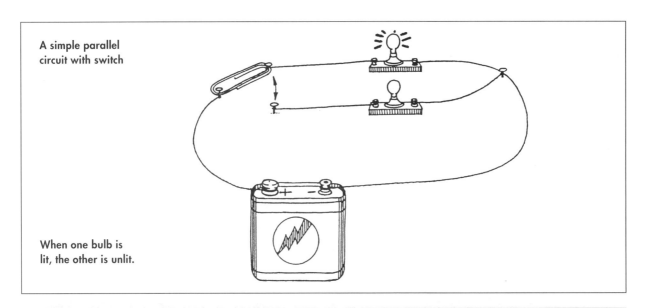

A simple parallel circuit with switch

When one bulb is lit, the other is unlit.

# Gadgets at Work

## Learning outcomes

### The programme considers:

- kitchen gadgets and their uses
- gadgets as aids to doing things
- kitchen design
- suitable materials for kitchen gadgets
- suitable materials for kitchenware
- materials that are heat insulators
- materials that are heat conductors
- use of conducting materials in kitchens
- use of insulating materials in kitchens
- kitchen safety.

**After viewing the programme and undertaking the activities suggested, pupils should have made progress in:**

### Knowledge and Understanding

▶ know about the need for rigorous safety procedures in kitchens

understand that materials are used for purposes appropriate to their properties

know that insulating relates to keeping things hot and also to keeping things cool

know that conductors transfer heat

understand the principles of fair testing

know how to set up a fair test.

### Skills and Techniques

▶ be able to test materials for their insulating properties

be able to design, make and test a variety of products for use in kitchens

be able to evaluate products for their usefulness and effectiveness.

### Attitudes and Values

▶ accept that rigorous safety practices are essential in kitchens

recognise the benefit of routines linked to safe practice.

## Programme synopsis

It is breakfast time in the McDonald household. There is lots of activity in the kitchen; machines and gadgets are at work. We look at kitchen designs, both domestic and commercial. The hazards of coping with hot surfaces and hot foods are pointed up. The presenter raises the question of why similar items of cutlery are made from different materials, e.g. why are some spoons metal and others wooden and others a mixture of metal and wood, or metal and plastic?

This leads into consideration of materials which conduct heat and materials which insulate from heat. The programme points up the dangers of using inappropriate cutlery and utensils for dealing with hot foods. There is discussion of the most suitable materials for making cosies and oven gloves. The safety rap points up the need to be careful when working in kitchens and handling kitchen equipment.

In the classroom, pupils design and make egg cosies and test them for their insulating properties. The programme stresses the need for tests to be fair tests, i.e. properly set up and executed.

Discussion of keeping heat in (cosies) and heat out (oven gloves) leads to consideration of materials used in freezers and refrigerators, the contents of which need to be insulated from external warmth. This leads to looking at the materials used to make drinking vessels, e.g. cups, mugs, glasses. Will each do equally well at keeping a drink cold or hot? All these things matter if people are to be safe; food is to be served as intended; and the proposed housewarming party is to be a success.

## Key vocabulary

gadgets, mechanisms, insulation, fair tests, utensils, equipment.

## Before the programme

▶ Discuss pupils' experience of working in kitchens, preparing food and cooking. What gadgets and utensils did they use? Did they make any silly mistakes in what they used and/or how they used it?

▶ Make a collection of kitchen gadgets. Include unusual and obscure items, and also items of historical interest. Have new gadgets made kitchen life easier?

▶ Discuss the need for safety in kitchens. Revise ideas on safety from previous programmes and add to those the need to be careful with hot foods and hot surfaces.

## During the programme

Pupils should be asked to view the programme with one or more of the following purposes in mind:

**1** Identify the parts of the programme in which materials with insulating properties are used.

**2** Identify potential safety hazards in relation to gadgets, equipment and hot foods (solids and liquids).

**3** Look for ideas for improving the design of gadgets or equipment used in kitchens.

## After the programme

The emphasis in this programme is on testing materials for their insulating properties. It is important that pupils know how to plan a fair test, i.e. all key variables, except for the one being tested, are held as constant as test conditions allow. Having collected and interpreted results from their testing, pupils should then put these results to practical use.

**1** All pupils should be given experience of devising a fair test, e.g. a test to discover which is the best egg cosy, oven glove, tea cosy.

**2** Individuals or groups of pupils can then go on to design, make and test one of the following products:

- an egg cosy to keep an egg warm. More than one material may be used.

- a container to keep ice-cubes cool.

- a cosy which will keep liquids hot in a pottery container.

**3** Make a collection of items that are heat insulators, and find out how they work, e.g. wine coolers, ice-packs, sleeping bags.

**4** In each case pupils should be asked to demonstrate their products and findings and to write a report. It is important that they come up with new ideas for items to design and test as well as testing old favourites, e.g. an ice cube insulator.

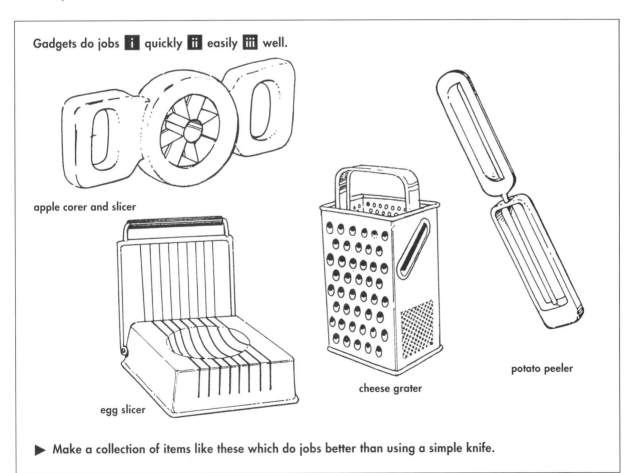

Gadgets do jobs **i** quickly **ii** easily **iii** well.

apple corer and slicer

egg slicer

cheese grater

potato peeler

▶ Make a collection of items like these which do jobs better than using a simple knife.

### RESOURCES

A collection of kitchen gadgets and materials used in kitchens, fabrics, foil, card, various glues, sewing machine, knitting wools and needles, sewing materials, insulating bags, bottles.

# Making for Success

## Learning outcomes

### The programme considers:

- planning a house warming party

- deciding what food and drink to buy

- designing and making food products and drinks

- large scale food production (pies, sweets, ice-cream)

- testing food and drink products

- setting up a classroom production line

- kitchen hygiene, kitchen safety

- classroom large-scale food production

- considering what makes a successful party.

**After viewing the programme and undertaking the activities suggested, pupils should have made progress in:**

### Knowledge and Understanding

▶ understand the need to plan production

know how factories plan production

know how a production line operates

understand that food preparation requires special attention to hygiene

understand that kitchens are potentially dangerous working environments.

### Skills and Techniques

▶ collect evidence of wants and needs

be able to draw up a plan for a party within certain guidelines

be able to design, make and test a number of food products

be able to set up a production line.

### Attitudes and Values

▶ appreciate that people are affected by their working environment

appreciate the satisfaction and also the frustration of being part of a production line

place a value on sound planning

place a value on health, safety and hygiene precautions.

## Programme synopsis

Mr and Mrs McDonald are scurrying about, shopping for their party. Some pies catch their eye.

We move to the pie-factory, and see the pies being mass produced and a new product being tested.

In school, pupils are also preparing for a party. The theme is to be 'Wheels'. They too have products to test, planning to do, and need a production line. The children make decorations, create menus, and design and produce foodstuffs around this theme.

Comparisons are drawn, and contrasts made, between the class activity and the bakery activity. We see the care that the children take over hygiene and safety. The safety rap is performed.

From party pastries we move to party sweets. Pupils are seen designing and making sweets and this is compared to, and contrasted with, sweet-making in a factory. The pupils prepare ice cream for the party.

The scene switches to the factory in which the ice cream is made, and the production process is explained.

Finally, we see the last-minute party preparations by the class and also by the McDonalds; and then the parties in action. Has all the careful planning and preparation paid off?

## Key vocabulary

factory, production line, safety and hygiene, task analysis, system.

## Before the programme

▶ Discuss with the class as a whole the sorts of things which have to be planned if a party is to be successful.

Ask them to think about the tasks which would need to be done. Ask them to suggest ways of deciding who would do each identified task.

The class will probably eventually want to allocate tasks on the basis either of personal willingness or of perceived aptitudes.

These are sound principles, but do make sure that pupils do not assume aptitudes on the basis of crude stereotyping – there should not be any such thing as 'girls' work' and 'boys' work'.

# During the programme

Pupils should be asked to view the programme with one or more of the following purposes in mind:

**1** Identify things to be considered when planning a party.

**2** Find out how a production line works.

**3** Find out how a company sets about introducing a new product.

**4** Identify safety and hygiene procedures necessary when handling food.

# After the programme

The emphasis of this programme is on the importance of sound collective planning and co-operative participation, without which no technological system, however advanced, can function adequately.

This programme would make ideal viewing at a time when a class intends to have a celebration. It could also be used by older pupils to prepare a party for younger children or for pensioners.

Preparation includes task identification and task allocation to groups and to individuals.

It is important that all pupils take part in the planning so that they have an opportunity to recognise the importance of correct sequencing of tasks and the gains which come from production lines, from specialisation and from proper monitoring of each stage of production.

Having drawn up the overall plan, the following (or similar) tasks can then be allocated, with responsibility being assigned to groups or individuals.

**1** Identify the wants and hopes of the large group which is to have the party.

**2** Design a production line for making pastry rolls or other savouries.

**3** Using production line techniques where appropriate: design, make and test a variety of foods and drinks. Prepare a sheet for evaluating them during the course of (or after) the party.

**4** Design and make the 'trimmings' for the party, including the invitations and decorations.

**5** Find out how factories make food products and identify the main differences between factory methods and classroom methods.

**6** Find out about food safety and hygiene regulations as applied to factories.

**7** Interview people who work in factories to find out about their specific tasks and how they feel about their work and their working conditions.

## A simple production flow chart

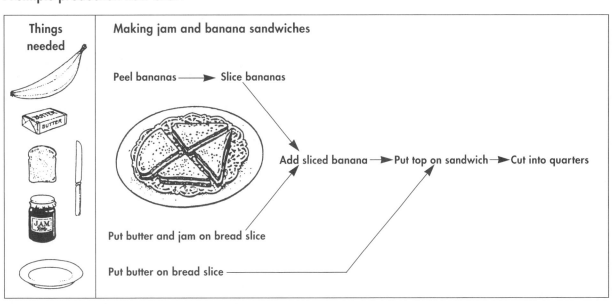

| Things needed | Making jam and banana sandwiches |
|---|---|

Peel bananas ⟶ Slice bananas

Add sliced banana ⟶ Put top on sandwich ⟶ Cut into quarters

Put butter and jam on bread slice

Put butter on bread slice

---

**RESOURCES**

Ingredients for food and drink products, magazines for ideas, recipe books, cooker, kitchen utensils, food wrapping materials, party 'trimmings'.

# Good Riddance

## Learning outcomes

**The programme considers:**

- rubbish/waste creation

- waste collection and disposal

- functional requirements of bins

- appropriate materials for bins

- appropriate bin designs

- health and safety aspects of rubbish collection and disposal

- environmental impact of rubbish

- opportunities for recycling

- land infill and reclamation.

**After viewing the programme and undertaking the activities suggested, pupils should have made progress in:**

### Knowledge and Understanding

▶ understand that waste collection and disposal is essential

understand the scale of the task

know about waste disposal processes

understand that waste collection and disposal involves costs

understand that bins, skips, etc. have specific functions

know that materials, design and construction are linked to bin function

know that materials, design and construction are linked to bin siting

understand the value of recycling

understand the benefits of litter reduction

know about health and safety aspects of rubbish collection and disposal.

## Skills and Techniques

▶ plan and carry out a litter survey in, e.g. school playground, street

design, make and test a litter container

design, make and test a piece of equipment for conveying rubbish

sift and sort categories of litter/waste

design and create anti-litter posters.

## Attitudes and Values

▶ recognise that people create litter

acknowledge the hazards of litter.

## Programme synopsis

On the McDonald's estate, it is refuse collection day. We see the wagon, and the waste to be collected. Inside the house, it is time to clear up the post-party mess.

We see the sacks, bins, skips that are needed for rubbish collection and waste recycling – all of them functionally designed using appropriate materials.

In a school, pupils examine rubbish receptacles and note their function, design and construction. With a class party in mind, they set about designing and making bins to meet specific needs in specific locations.

The school's refuse is collected. We see it compacted, and taken to a landfill site. Will this site really be a park one day?

Back at the school, pupils test their bins to see if they will perform the job they were designed and made to do; and enjoy mixed success.

## Key vocabulary

litter, rubbish (trash, waste), recycling, landfill sites, receptacles.

# Before the programme

Make sure that you know colloquialisms relating to rubbish collection and disposal. Your pupils may well use them in referring to scenes in the programme.

Pupils will benefit from seeing parts of the programme several times. Make sure that you have obtained a video-recording of it so that it can be replayed.

▶ Find out what pupils already know about local refuse collection/disposal, e.g. mode, frequency, receptacles, limitations on customer use, bye-laws.

▶ Identify pupils who have recently held a party. What rubbish was generated? How was it disposed of? Were arrangements made to recycle any of it? Did the party-giver(s) think to plan in advance for the collection and disposal of rubbish?

▶ Find out what the pupils' attitude is towards litter. Do they think it matters?

▶ Identify the main sources of rubbish and litter within the school.

▶ Carry out a litter survey of the school playground. Design a recording sheet on which can be noted:

[a] types of litter, e.g. paper, metal

[b] probable source of litter, e.g. tuck shop.

# After the programme

This programme concentrates on the organising and planning that goes into successful refuse collection and disposal. Planning includes design and location of receptacles and vehicles, provision for regular emptying/collection, proper operation of disposal and recycling facilities.

Technology can achieve a lot, but at a cost. Emphasis therefore has to be placed on minimising waste and reducing litter. The most successful refuse collection campaign may well be the one that shows the biggest fall in demand for the service, rather than the one which results in the most collecting and disposing.

Groups and/or individuals should tackle one or more of the following tasks:

**1** Find out about the disposal of school rubbish; how it is sorted and where it is dumped. Construct a chart to show your findings.

**2** Organise an anti-litter campaign within the school. Design suitable posters and suggest possible incentives for pupils and staff to reduce school litter.

**3** Organise a recycling campaign within the school. Make sure that you check school regulations about storage.

**4** Organise a daily collection of the indoor school rubbish from the classroom over a week. Sort and classify the materials which make up the rubbish. Present your findings to the whole school.

**5** Design, make and test a rubbish receptacle for classroom use.

**6** Do a survey of outdoor litter bins to find out which types are the most effective. List any major problems and write to the relevant companies giving your findings.

**7** Make a list of the safety rules which should be followed when handling rubbish.

This topic lends itself to involving the whole school. It may be used by older pupils to engage all the pupils in the school in nurturing their school environment.

---

You will find further exercises related to recycling and rubbish disposal in Living With Technology: Pupils' Worksheets. For further details, see the inside back cover.

---

## RESOURCES

Camera, paper, plastic, cardboard, various glues, staples, hinges, tools for cutting and shaping materials, a collection of containers used as receptacles for rubbish.

# Street Wise

## Learning outcomes

### The programme considers:

- what is meant by street furniture
- developments over time in the design of postboxes
- the role of postboxes within the postal system
- a manufacturing process using moulds and castings
- developments over time in the design of telephone boxes
- how technology, past and present, responds to changing human needs
- the properties of materials that make them useful for certain purposes
- changes and developments in street lighting
- control systems for street lights
- light pollution.

**After viewing the programme and undertaking the activities suggested, pupils should have made progress in:**

### Knowledge and Understanding

▶ understand the importance of good design in creating functional objects

understand that good design can extend a product's useful working life

understand that advances in technology make new designs possible

understand that changes in people's requirements lead to changes in design

understand that advances in technology influence the design of street furniture

know some of the changes that have been made to the design of street furniture

know how the postal system operates

understand the basic processes involved in making moulds and producing castings

know some of the advantages of automated control systems

know how control technology is used to operate street lighting systems

know some of the other consequences of introducing new technology, e.g. job changes and cutbacks.

## Skills and Techniques

▶ plan, design and build a model of a postbox for the year 2000

identify key requirements and constraints before designing objects

evaluate designs in relation to their effectiveness

collect and record evidence of street furniture using sketches and photographs

carry out a survey and use a computer data base to retrieve relevant information.

## Attitudes and Values

▶ appreciate the need for designers and manufacturers to respond to pressures for change

appreciate the impact of good design on users

appreciate the impact of good and bad design on the environment

recognise that care must be taken to take account of wider environmental issues, e.g. light pollution, pavement clutter, when designing and installing street furniture.

## Programme synopsis

The two presenters (Claire and John) go out and about to look at street furniture, and ask us to consider its functions and how it has developed over time.

Recent changes in postboxes are shown. Failures and successes with early designs are recounted and illustrated. We then see some of the different stages that make up the postal system (collection, sorting, franking, distribution, delivery) and look at an example of how, with the help of new designs and new technology, the postal system is changing to meet the changing needs of consumers.

The programme then looks at how postboxes are made, using a well-established casting process on which modern technology has had comparatively little impact. In a foundry, we see moulds being made, boxes being cast, flashings being removed, and postboxes being assembled and painted.

The programme then looks at the design of public telephone boxes. The complexities and drawbacks of old-style telephones and telephone boxes are discussed and compared with their modern counterparts. The influence of new materials and new approaches is clearly illustrated.

The programme then looks at the design of street lights. Again, old and new are compared. We see how technology has helped bring street lighting a long way from the early gas lamps to today's photo-electrically controlled street lighting systems. The problem of light pollution is raised, and we are asked to consider how it might be tackled.

As a final thought, the presenters ask whether the piecemeal proliferation of street furniture has produced a clutter which calls for the layout of streets and pavements to be rethought and replanned.

## Key vocabulary

street furniture, design, postbox, pillar box, system, postal system, solution, casting, efficient, cast iron, mould, core, reproduction furniture, lamp post, telephone box, gas lamps, photo-electric, cell, automatic, pollution.

## Before the programme

▶ Ask pupils what they think is meant by 'furniture'. Where would they normally expect to come across furniture? Do they have furniture outside their homes, e.g. garden furniture?

▶ What sorts of things are to be found standing on or built into the roads and pavements of streets in Britain? Have pupils passed any of them on their way to school? Can these be thought of as furniture?

▶ Inform pupils that the programme discusses how these everyday objects come to be on our streets and how and why they have changed over the years.

## During the programme

The programme consists of several sections. Pupils could be given different tasks.

1 Identify the main considerations that have influenced the design of postboxes.

2 Look carefully at the main stages in the manufacture of a postbox.

3 Note the main changes in the design of public telephones and public telephone boxes.

4 Identify changes in the way that street lights are switched on and off.

## After the programme

The emphasis of this programme is on changes in the design of commonplace street items that meet everyday public needs. The programme illustrates changes in their design and construction which changing customer needs have made necessary and which developments in design and advances in technology have made possible.

Several themes run through the programme, and questions and issues are raised that could be considered by the class in follow-up activities.

1 Research the different designs of postboxes that are still in use in Britain today. Produce a poster illustrating the different designs and explaining why there is more than one standard design.

2 Bearing in mind the changing needs of customers, design and construct a model of a postbox suitable to meet people's needs in the year 2000.

3 Using a questionnaire of your own design, collect information about the different types of mail (e.g. size, shape, fragility, purpose, urgency, solicited, unsolicited) that are delivered to pupils' homes. Use a computer database to collate and display the data gathered.

4 Produce a design for a street light which sheds most of its light downwards in order to lessen light pollution.

5 Suggest reasons why some people might want to retain some of the old designs of street furniture.

6 This programme could be used as part of a local study. A field trip would enable pupils to investigate street furniture in their own locality. Several activities could evolve from this.

a On a street map or plan, record the position and type of items of street furniture, using a key.

b Take rubbings of details that have been produced as part of a casting or other manufacturing process. Jot down possible reasons why this detail has been included in the design.

c Make sketches, take them back to the classroom and use them either as illustrations to accompany written tasks or as artwork.

d Measure the dimensions of items of street furniture and consider the space that they take up, e.g. Is the space well used? What proportion of a pavement is lost?

e Take photographs of items of street furniture, and make notes on the suitability of their size and position. For example, is the object useful to blind people or merely a danger to them?

### RESOURCES

Maps, plans, computer, database program, camera, rubbing crayons, paper, tape measure.

New technology has transformed street lighting.

# Water Works

## Learning outcomes

### The programme considers:

- clean water as a vital resource

- how water is supplied to homes

- materials used for water pipes

- water storage and plumbing in the home

- self-regulating water devices e.g. flush toilets

- the ways in which households use water

- the role of technology in improving water supply and distribution

- the role of design and technology in promoting water conservation.

**After viewing the programme and undertaking the activities suggested, pupils should have made progress in:**

### Knowledge and Understanding

▶ understand that materials are used for purposes appropriate to their properties

   understand how water is stored and pumped

   understand how water can be recycled and purified

   know some of the means by which water supplies can be conserved

   understand the need to save energy and conserve natural resources.

### Skills and Techniques

▶ plan, design and build models to illustrate the movement/flow of a water siphon, high pressure, U-bend, etc.

   collect and display data

   create and label simple sketches and diagrams.

### Attitudes and Values

▶ appreciate the need to conserve water

   be aware of how water, or the lack of it, affects the quality of people's lives

   appreciate the contribution made by technology to water conservation programmes.

## Programme synopsis

In Britain, most of us take water for granted – it is always there, at no apparent cost and at the turn of a tap. But how does it get there? The presenters take us below the street to examine the mains water pipes and the network of branch pipes which provides each household with a clean water supply. We learn how new technology is helping to make underground pipe maintenance, repair and replacement easier.

We consider the properties of materials used to make modern water pipes and also the materials used in the past, and their deficiencies. In the Eureka! Museum in Halifax, a modern system of water moving through a network of pipes is contrasted with methods used in developing countries, including an Archimedes' screw.

With the help of graphics, Claire explains the self-regulating system built into flush toilets, and contrasts it with methods of sewage disposal used in the past. The presenters outline the main ways in which a British household uses water, and look at how households might set about using less water in the face of higher prices for metered water, which reflect the spiralling costs of its collection, storage, purification and distribution.

The focus switches to dishwashers and washing machines, which are timesaving but are also water-guzzlers. The programme shows how manufacturers are developing new designs intended to do just as good a job but using less water.

Finally, the programme considers the cost of providing clean water in a society where there is a growing demand for water, and asks whether, in spite of many technological advances, the UK can afford to keep increasing its demand for water.

## Key vocabulary

high pressure, hydrant, water closet, joints, cast iron, lead, copper, stop-tap, sewage, cistern, sensor, probe, sound waves, gravity, Archimedes' screw, flush toilet, sewage system, cistern, self-regulating, half flush, pressure switch, drum, natural resources.

An illustration of an Archimedes' screw is included in the Pupils' Worksheets (see inside back cover).

# Before the programme

**1** Discuss with pupils their own experience of water services, i.e. how and when they use them.

**2** Find out their level of awareness of the water system in their own home, e.g. where does the water supply enter the house, how is it turned off?

**3** Quiz them on their awareness of water being piped underground. Have they any experience of leaks, burst water mains, blocked drains, hydrants in use, etc?

**4** Give background information about the development of the W.C.. Discuss the link between water contamination and disease.

**5** Make a collection of pictures and references to items of historical interest, e.g. early adverts for washing machines, baths, chamber pots.

**6** Estimate the volume of water used daily by each person.

# During the programme

Pupils should be asked to view the programme with one or more of the following purposes in mind.

**1** Note how water is supplied to homes.

**2** Identify a number of uses for water in and around the home.

**3** Note ways of conserving water e.g. shower v bath.

**4** Look for ideas for improving the design of water-using machines.

# After the programme

**1** Ask each pupil to draw a sketchplan of their home, and mark on it (a) the place where the water supply enters the house (b) the stop-tap (c) the places where there are water outlets, e.g. taps, shower-heads, hoses attached to washing machines, etc.. Create a graph to show the number of water outlets in typical and less typical homes.

**2** Identify the materials used to provide an underground water supply. List the advantages and disadvantages of each.

**3** Arrange a class visit to a local water authority. Alternatively, ask someone from the water authority to visit the school.

**4** Think of ways of collecting water, e.g. set up a water butt to collect rainwater. Use it to water garden or pot plants. Devise a way of measuring the amount of water collected.

**5** Find out about water-lifting devices used in developing countries for irrigation. Plan, design and build a device to lift a bucketful of water.

**6** Debate whether or not charging people directly for the water they use will encourage them to use less of it.

**7** Design a siphon and/or a solar still.

**8** Collect, display, and read brochures about water-saving materials and devices.

---
### RESOURCES

Measuring cylinders, measuring jugs, plastic tubing, washing-up bottles, simple water tray pump.

---

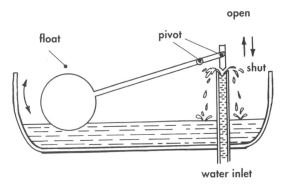

A domestic toilet flush system is self-regulating but not self-starting. Why is it self-regulating? Why isn't it self-starting?

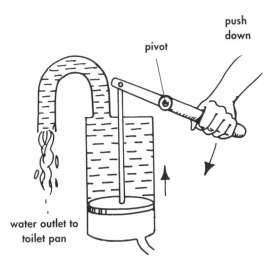

# Safe Ways

## Learning outcomes

### The programme considers:

- the impact of motorised transport on the speed and safety of road travel

- ways and means of improving safety for pedestrians, cyclists and drivers

- the conflicting needs of particular groups of road users

- traffic control systems

- design and planning of road networks

- the design of artefacts intended to create safer roads e.g. road signs, crossings, barriers, speed impeders

- the environmental impact of traffic

- the police role in monitoring traffic and enforcing traffic regulations

- the role of technology in modern policing of roads

- the importance of educating road users.

**After viewing the programme and undertaking the activities suggested, pupils should have made progress in:**

### Knowledge and Understanding

▶ know a range of causes of road accidents

know some ways of reducing the number and severity of road accidents

understand the role of crash barriers in accident prevention

understand the role played by testing and evaluation in creating safer roads

know how technology is used to monitor and control traffic movement

be aware of different technologies used to detect and record speeding motorists

understand that road designers need to take into account the conflicting needs of different groups of road users

understand that new technology is seen as a major contributor to safer roads.

### Skills and Techniques

▶ monitor and collect evidence of traffic volumes and movement near the school

extract information from different sources about road and vehicle safety

plan a basic road crossing system to take account of the needs of different groups of road users

using model cars, design and carry out experiments to evaluate the effect of speed on stopping distance and impact damage.

### Attitudes and Values

▶ recognise that people contribute to accidents

recognise that people can contribute to improved levels of road safety

develop a sense of responsibility towards the safety of themselves and others when using roads

appreciate the beneficial role of the police in relation to improving road safety

recognise and accept the role played by technology in improving road safety

recognise and accept the contribution of design and planning to the creation of safer, more environmentally friendly road systems

## Programme synopsis

The presenter refers to a time when pedestrians and horsedrawn traffic dominated the roads, and outlines the impact of cars on road design. The programme then considers the need for road systems to adapt to the requirements of drivers making longer, faster journeys. We are shown how higher road speeds have led to attempts to separate traffic and pedestrians.

We look at some of the dangers associated with roads, particularly for children, and the part played by good design in, for example, the provision of road crossings.

The programme establishes the need to control the movement of vehicles and people, and emphasizes the different needs of different groups of road users. The presenters then look at different ways of controlling traffic, with particular reference to the work of designers in devising ways and means of causing traffic to slow down.

We then have a chance to compare different designs of crash barriers and consider how new designs making use of new technology have been used to improve the performance of crash barriers.

With the help of a police patrol, we learn about what is being done to encourage drivers to drive within the requirements of the law and about the role of modern technology in enforcing the law.

The programme ends by noting that the number of motor vehicles using the road network continues to increase, and suggests that further traffic control systems will have to be devised, developed and implemented.

## Key vocabulary

transport, emergency, traffic controls, barriers, safety, motorway, dual carriageway, by-pass, pedestrian, visibility, offsetting, warning signs, speed, detector, road conditions, concrete, stopping power, absorb, impact, extruded, campaign, sensor, signalling system, radar.

## Before the programme

▶ Find out what pupils already know about the early development of roads and road transport.

▶ Ask pupils to give their views on the main factors that lead to roads being safe or unsafe
(a) for pedestrians to use, (b) for cyclists to use, (c) for drivers to use.

▶ Discuss why there is a need to improve road safety in Britain.

▶ Make a collection of pictures and news cuttings relating to roads, road markings, road signs, road improvement schemes, etc.

## During the programme

Pupils should be asked to view the programme with one or more of the following purposes in mind:

1 Identify some of the main causes of road accidents involving pedestrians.

2 Look for measures taken to reduce the speed of vehicles using the roads.

3 Consider the importance of correct choice of materials in the manufacture of road signs, road markings, etc.

4 Look for the main influences on the design of crash barriers.

## After the programme

The overall emphasis of the programme is on road safety, and on the contribution that good design, sound planning and judicious use of modern technology can make to road safety.

1 Look for evidence locally of previous modes of transport (e.g pack horse) and early transport routes (e.g drove roads, military roads). Bring them to the pupils' notice.

2 Making use of all sources at your disposal, including contact with car manufacturers and suppliers and other suitable sources identified by your pupils, research recent design features intended to improve vehicle safety.

3 Invite a police road safety representative to talk to the class or school on the role of the police in improving road safety.

4 Discuss how the needs of different groups in society (e.g children, elderly, the disabled) may be catered for in the design and layout of a pedestrian crossing. Study a local crossing point, and assess how well it meets the needs of people who are likely to use it.

5 Survey traffic flows at different sites outside the school at different times of day. Collate the information in a computer database. Use the data to identify the most dangerous time(s) of day for pedestrians to be on roads near the school. When doing your survey, make a note of any examples of dangerous behaviour by either drivers or pedestrians.

6 Plan and design a system to control traffic flows at a point where cattle have to cross a road twice a day to be milked. Use signs, road markings, sounds, etc.

7 Use model vehicles and ramps to investigate: the effect of speed on a vehicle's stopping distance; the effect of speed on impact damage, e.g. penetration into modelling material.

8 Use Lego Technic to build a model set of traffic lights which operate in the correct sequence at a crossroads.

| RESOURCES |
| --- |
| Model cars, Lego Technic, soft modelling material, computer database program. |

Advances in car design aimed at improving safety deserve a programme to themselves.

# Park and Ride

## Learning outcomes

### The programme considers:

- taking account of the needs of people with disabilities when planning the layout and furnishings of play areas, fun parks and the like

- basic structures used to support playground furniture

- different ways of transmitting energy and motion (rotational, vertical, lateral)

- use of mechanisms to move large structures

- methods of simulating movement, e.g. of a car

- the role of technology in making forms of play more exciting, safer and more accessible to all.

**After viewing the programme and undertaking the activities suggested, pupils should have made progress in:**

### Knowledge and Understanding

▶ understand that disabled people have particular needs that deserve to be considered when designing play areas and equipment

know the basic shapes and structures used to support playground equipment

know that energy from a push can be transmitted in different ways

know that belts, pulleys, chains, cogs, gears and pistons are different ways of passing on movement

understand that playgrounds are potentially dangerous

understand the contribution that good design can make to the safety of play areas

know that simulated movement can be a source of safe and exciting play.

### Skills and Techniques

▶ test materials for their cushioning and durability properties

interview disabled people and collect evidence of their wants and needs

plan a playground to take account of safety and people's abilities

make a basic, tall but stable structure out of straws.

## Attitudes and Values

▶ accept the need to provide play facilities for everyone, including people with disabilities

appreciate how developments in technology may influence play and leisure experiences.

## Programme synopsis

The presenter visits an adventure playground, and points out important factors that have to be considered when planning the layout, designing the equipment, and choosing the construction materials.

We look at the kinds of movement found in standard playground furniture and consider whether it would be easy for someone in a wheelchair to use it. The programme then takes us to an adventure playground that has been designed to meet the needs of disabled people.

In Aberdeen, John demonstrates ways of passing on movement, so that large objects, such as fairground rides, can be made to move using pulleys, chains, pistons, etc. At Alton Towers, we see the general layout and look at the design features that give access for disabled people. We then experience various rides in action, including Nemesis, Congo Rapids and the Magic Carpet. Claire, Julie (in a wheelchair) and Terry (her companion) discuss the suitability of some of these rides for wheelchair users. The design features that make the structures strong are pointed out, and are compared with the design features of smaller rides.

In an attempt to find something exciting that someone in a wheelchair could use easily, John looks at a car simulator. Whilst the on-screen effects are good, the user feels little or no sense of movement. This leads into a study of ways of making simulators move convincingly. Hydraulic and electro-magnetic systems of creating movement are compared, with the help of inventor Phillip Denne.

The programme ends with a taster of Virtual Reality, a ground-breaking technology that opens up the prospect of new safe ways of having fun in the comfort of one's own home. The presenters ask whether these new developments are likely to spell the end of traditional playgrounds, playparks, fairgrounds, amusement parks; or will the firm favourites of today and yesteryear find ways of continuing to attract customers?

# Key vocabulary

playground furniture, structures, stable, balance, pivot, gravity, mechanisms, transmit, movement, power, machinery, pulley, cog, chain, piston, hydraulics.

## Before the programme

▶ Discuss with pupils their experiences of playgrounds, both small and large scale.

▶ With help from pupils, draw up a list of the kinds of movement experienced on rides in playgrounds and playparks, e.g. rotating, up and down, side to side, sliding, shaking.

▶ In relation to playparks etc. known to them, consider with pupils the suitability of playground furniture and rides for people with disabilities.

## During the programme

Pupils should be asked to view the programme with one or more of the following purposes in mind:

1 Identify factors which are important when planning a play area.

2 Identify potential dangers within a play area.

3 Identify the forms of propulsion that are now used to create fun experiences.

4 Note apparatus and equipment that is suitable for those with disabilities and look for ideas for redesigning or developing equipment to make it suitable for people with disabilities.

5 Identify the different kinds of motion featured in the programme and think of new ideas for rides which incorporate one or more of these kinds of motion.

## After the programme

The programme shows the increase in complexity and scale of playground equipment made possible by new materials and the application of new ideas allied to new technology. The programme also emphasizes the importance of aiming to ensure that most people, be they elderly, small, large or disabled, can use at least some of the equipment. That aim is achieved by careful designing of the furniture, by planning the area, and through staff training. These are the themes picked up in the suggested follow-up activities.

1 Pupils, in groups, should devise and carry out a fair test to determine which range of materials is safest as ground cover around and beneath playground furniture.

2 Other pupils, in groups, should devise and carry out a fair test to investigate the durability of the same materials used in Activity 1 above.

3 The two sets of pupils should compare their results. They should then be asked to discuss whether there is a material that can do both jobs well, or whether a compromise has to be reached.

4 Pupils should experiment with a metre stick as a see-saw (lever) and compare the relationship between the length of see-saw either side of the pivot point and the weight needed on either side of the see-saw to balance it. They should then discuss the relevance of what they have discovered to see-saw design and the safe use of see-saws.

5 Pupils can interview people with special needs to find out their requirements in a playground. They can then discuss how these needs could be met when redesigning a replacement for a common piece of play equipment such as a roundabout.

6 Given a set amount of straws, pupils can design and construct a tower which is as high as possible but stable enough to support a prescribed weight.

### RESOURCES

Samples of materials to be tested as potential surfaces for play areas; straws.

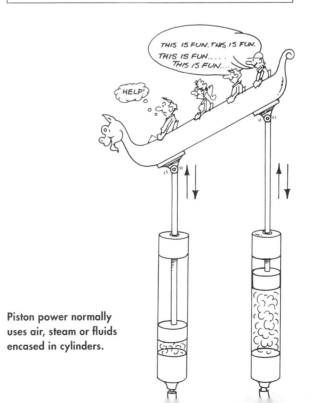

Piston power normally uses air, steam or fluids encased in cylinders.

# On the Ball

## Learning outcomes

### The programme considers:

- the development of balls and ball games

- materials used in making balls, particularly footballs and tennis balls

- the properties needed in footballs and tennis balls at different levels of each game

- the design and development of merchandise linked to a professional football team

- the design, production and use of logos

- manufacture of stitched and moulded footballs, and of tennis balls

- testing and quality control of footballs and tennis balls

- futuristic sports balls.

**After viewing the programme and undertaking the activities suggested, pupils should have made progress in:**

### Knowledge and Understanding

▶ understand that the rules and requirements of a particular sport or game influence the design and construction of the equipment it uses

understand that changes in technology can influence how a game is played

know how some sportsballs are manufactured

understand that ball manufacture involves research, design, production, testing and evaluation

know some of the skills used in making a ball

understand the importance of quality control in the manufacturing process

understand the importance placed on the consistency of a ball's performance

know that the condition of a ball affects its performance.

### Skills and Techniques

▶ able to design sports equipment and clothing to incorporate a company logo

able to devise and use a questionnaire for a survey of financial sponsorship in sport

able to plan and carry out experiments to evaluate the effects on performance criteria of adjusting the condition of the ball

able to plan and compile a poster giving illustrated information about a ball.

### Attitudes and Values

▶ care about and appreciate the quality of design and production of sports equipment

acknowledge and appreciate the skills associated with playing ball games well.

## Programme synopsis

The presenter points out that a sports ball is designed to meet the demands of a particular sport or game, so one kind of sports ball may well not suit the rules and needs of other sports or games. There follows a brief account of the development of balls and ball games, and an old football is used to illustrate changes in design, materials used and construction that have occurred in the course of time.

We visit a factory in Huddersfield, watch footballs being made and see a stitcher at work. Then we visit a professional football club, where modern professional footballers describe and demonstrate the qualities they expect a match-quality football to have. The presenter explains why football manufacturers produce a wide range of footballs of different grades.

We learn about the importance to sports equipment manufacturers of establishing a wide range of products and of ensuring maximum publicity for their products. We see examples of how a product range is developed, and are shown the part that good design plays in making sure that a firm's products are widely recognised.

The programme then looks at the manufacturing process that produces moulded footballs of a type used in schools. We then see the balls being tried and tested, both in the factory and on the sports field.

A study of tennis ball manufacture allows useful comparisons to be made and contrasts to be noted. As with football, the game's legislators have clear ideas about what a tennis ball must be able to do consistently. We see tennis balls being tested to see if they meet these requirements.

Finally, the presenters show us some recent developments in ball design and construction for newly-invented games, and they speculate about what the ball and ball game of the future might look like.

## Key vocabulary

materials, reacted, synthetic, leather, client, design, logo, sponsorship, forming, bladder, moulded, offcuts, recycling, inflatable, textured surface, professional, amateur, racquet, quality control.

## Before the programme

1 Put on display a ball used in the game or sport that is most popular with your pupils. Ask pupils to give reasons why they think the ball is good or poor from their point of view as players of that game.

2 Ask some pupils to bring in the ball each uses when playing their favourite sport. For each ball, let pupils study its construction (without damaging it!) and the materials from which it is made. Ask a pupil to tell the class what a skilful player can make the ball do within the rules of the game in which it is used.

3 If footballs and tennis balls have not featured so far, display each in turn and ask pupils what makes a football and/or a tennis ball 'a good one' from their point of view as players/users. List the properties of good footballs and good tennis balls.

4 Find out what pupils understand by a logo.

5 Find out what pupils know and understand about sponsorship in sport.

6 Make a list of brand names or 'messages' which the pupils associate, through sponsorship, with sport, sports teams, or sporting personalities.

## During the programme

Groups of pupils can be assigned particular tasks, e.g.

1 Look and listen out for what professional footballers expect of a football.

2 Identify the forms of ball-testing seen in the programme.

3 Note what is needed to design a successful logo.

## After the programme

1 Compile a list of games or sports that use a ball.

2 With the help of the pupils, decide which ball in common use seems to be the most versatile in terms of the range of games that can be played with it.

3 Decide which ball seems to be the most versatile in terms of the range of things a skilful player can get it to do as part of playing a particular game or sport.

4 Select one, two or three balls. Design a poster, illustrating each ball, with a view to boosting its sales. Add labels that point out the main features of each ball, e.g. the material(s) from which it is made.

5 Using a football, devise some simple training routines. Then attempt the same routines with other balls such as a tennis ball, a basketball, a rugby ball. Comment on the benefits or problems resulting from the ball's different characteristics, e.g, size, shape, hardness.

6 Choose a sports league. Conduct research to find out the sponsors and their products associated with the teams in that league. Categorise the findings and, after discussion, present them in an appropriate format.

7 Design and carry out experiments to find out how the bounce of a football reacts to changes in the ball's temperature and/or pressure.

8 Decide which is your favourite ball-using sport. For that sport, design 'the ball of the future', firstly as you personally would like it to be, and secondly as you think it is likely to be. Explain to the rest of the class the reasons why you selected your two designs.

9 Invent a ball game and design a ball to suit the game and its rules. Describe the properties of the ball.

10 Select a ball-playing sport for which your school has a school team. With the help of sports catalogues, estimate the cost of providing the team with training and match balls for a season. Decide what other information you will need before you can start this task.

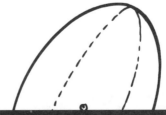

### RESOURCES

An assortment of sports balls, pump with pressure gauge, metre sticks, paper, crayons.

# Helpful Hints

## Building for strength

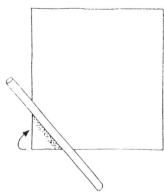

Roll paper around a cane or doweling rod from corner to corner. Stick the paper roll with a strong water-based glue. Remove the doweling. You have a strong tube.

Triangular shapes add strength. This rectangular wooden frame has been strengthened by fixing triangular card to each corner.

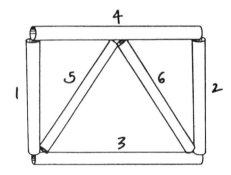

Vertical tubes (1,2) are strong. Horizontal tubes (3,4) are weaker, and need support (5,6).

Tubular bundles of tubes make very strong structures.

### Electrical circuits

For connecting up circuits, there is a preferred order which will help avoid unwanted short circuits:

Connect wires to the output (the bulb)

Connect wires to the source (the battery)

Note where a switch is placed: in the wire that leads from the live terminal of the source (the battery) to the output (the bulb).

**Living with Technology**    4 S C H O O L S

# A fun application of a simple circuit

## Shaky hand tester

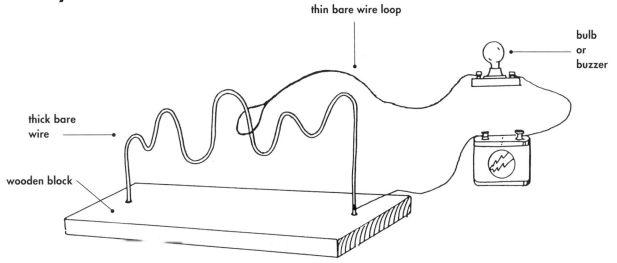

thin bare wire loop

bulb
or
buzzer

thick bare
wire

wooden block

# Making an electromagnet

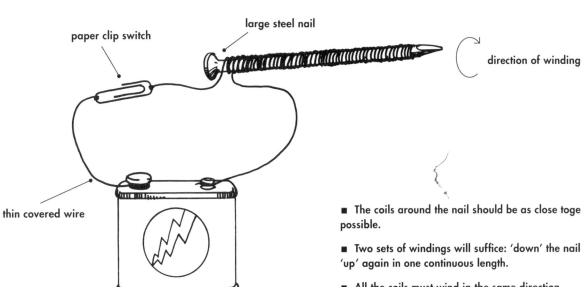

paper clip switch

large steel nail

direction of winding

thin covered wire

■ The coils around the nail should be as close together as possible.

■ Two sets of windings will suffice: 'down' the nail and back 'up' again in one continuous length.

■ All the coils must wind in the same direction.

**When the switch is used to complete the circuit, the nail will become magnetised.**

▶ Pupils can suggest how to test that the nail really has become a magnet.

▶ They can see what happens to the magnetism in the nail when the circuit is broken.

▶ They should try this out with nails made from different sorts of metal.

▶ Ask pupils to think how designers might make use of the movement that happens (a) when metals are attracted to a magnet, (b) when something that is a magnet stops being a magnet. If they are unable to come up with any ideas, let them watch the programme **Park and Ride** again. Those pupils who have train sets can study any electrically-operated points these may have.

4
S C H O O L S    **Living with Technology**

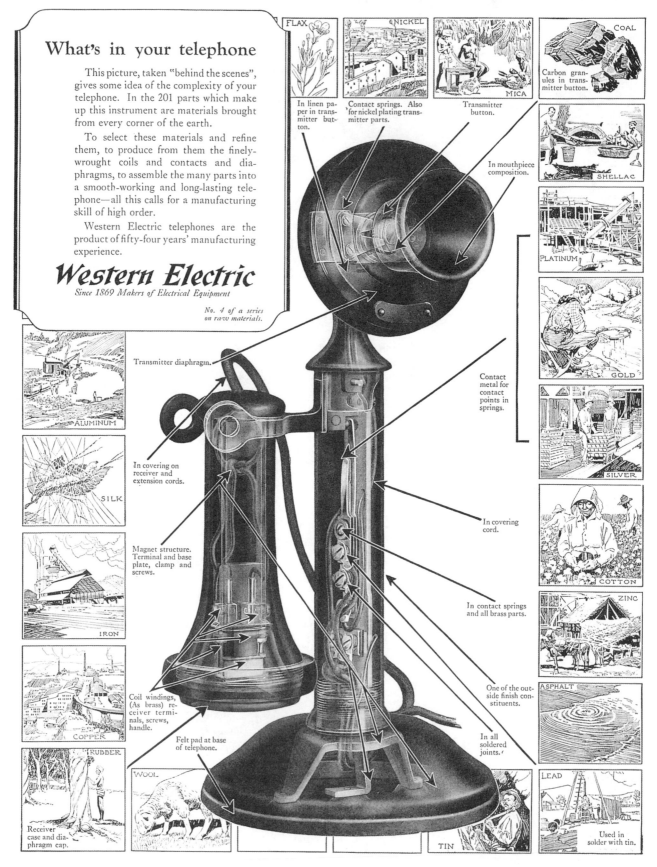

## What's in your telephone

This picture, taken "behind the scenes", gives some idea of the complexity of your telephone. In the 201 parts which make up this instrument are materials brought from every corner of the earth.

To select these materials and refine them, to produce from them the finely-wrought coils and contacts and diaphragms, to assemble the many parts into a smooth-working and long-lasting telephone—all this calls for a manufacturing skill of high order.

Western Electric telephones are the product of fifty-four years' manufacturing experience.

### Western Electric
Since 1869 Makers of Electrical Equipment

No. 4 of a series
on raw materials.

FLAX — In linen paper in transmitter button.

NICKEL — Contact springs. Also for nickel plating transmitter parts.

Transmitter button. MICA

COAL — Carbon granules in transmitter button.

In mouthpiece composition.

SHELLAC

PLATINUM

GOLD

Contact metal for contact points in springs.

SILVER

COTTON

ZINC

In covering cord.

In contact springs and all brass parts.

ASPHALT — One of the outside finish constituents.

In all soldered joints.

LEAD — Used in solder with tin.

Transmitter diaphragm.

In covering on receiver and extension cords.

Magnet structure. Terminal and base plate, clamp and screws.

ALUMINUM

SILK

IRON

COPPER

Coil windings, (As brass) receiver terminals, screws, handle.

Felt pad at base of telephone.

RUBBER — Receiver case and diaphragm cap.

WOOL

TIN

Since it was first invented, the telephone has changed in appearance, construction, component parts and its method of operation. The system, of which it is a part and within which it has to fit, has greatly changed. There has also been an upsurge in its ownership and use. With the rapid expansion of 'add-on' features, and with the introduction of videophones, the telephone is due to change again. Yet its key function remains unaltered.

**Living with Technology**

4 SCHOOLS

# Then and Now

Some pupils will struggle to understand the forces which bring about technological change over time. However, given objects to look at and/or handle, all pupils are able to agree that change has taken place.

Below are questions that pupils can ask themselves about any product of which they have seen an old and a current version. You may wish your more able pupils to phrase their own questions and set up their own lines of enquiry. It is likely, however, that some of your pupils would welcome being given the sheet below as a 'way in'. They can add other questions of their own. For some products, some questions will be redundant.

If old versions of things are not obtainable, pictures of them can generate discussion when set against the modern article.

If telephones hold little interest, then you could always try bed warmers, tin openers, shoe polish, lawn mowers, clocks, watches, radio sets, pens, irons, football boots, railway locos. If you decide to photocopy this sheet, you can create space for pupils to draw sketches by covering up this top section.

This exercise encompasses many of the areas of technology itemised on Page 3 of this guide.

| | The old | The new |
|---|---|---|
| 1 What is it called? | | |
| 2 What is it for? | | |
| 3 What extra features does it have? | | |
| 4 'A luxury in its time'. True? False? | | |
| 5 What materials is it made from? | | |
| 6 How easy is it to use? | | |
| 7 How is it mainly held together? | | |
| 8 How easy would it be for the owner to take it apart? | | |
| 9 How well does it do what it was designed to do? | | |
| 10 How strong does it seem? | | |
| 11 What are the main differences between the old one and the new one? | | |
| 12 Which one would you rather have to use? | | |
| 13 Why? | | |

27

# Further Information

## Select bibliography

### Books

**Starting Technology: Electricity** (Wayland)
ISBN 0-7502-0169-X

**Exploring Technology: Houses and Homes** (Wayland)
ISBN 0-7502-0211-4

**Exploring Technology: Structures** (Wayland)
ISBN 0-85210-932-7

**Design and Technology 5 – 12** by Pat Williams and
David Jinks (The Falmer Press) ISBN 1-85000-049-2

**Let's Do Science; Batteries, Bulbs and Circuits**
(Edward Arnold) ISBN 0-7131-0905-X

**Design and Technology through Problem Solving**
(Simon and Schuster) ISBN 0-7501-0032-X

**Let's Make It Work Book 2** (Macmillan)
ISBN 0-333-44025-0

**Let's Make It Work Teachers' Guide**
ISBN 0-333-48092-9

**Telephone Boxes** by Neil Johannessen
(Shire Publications) ISBN 0-7478-0250-5

### Kits

**Tactic** NES Arnold, Galt, Heron

**Teko** Osmiroid, NES Arnold

**Lego Technic II 1032** (which includes a motor),
NES Arnold

## Places to visit

For insights into technology past and present, possible
visits include:

- **Local firms,** including local newspapers, that have
been pre-visited and properly briefed. Even if the old
machinery and methods have disappeared, there is
usually someone more than willing to tell you about
them. Health and safety regulations may preclude
certain types of visit.

- **Museums** built around the general theme of How
We Used to Live. This includes museums dedicated,
for example, not only to Victorians but also to
Romans, Vikings, Greeks and Egyptians.

- **Museums** devoted in whole or in part to science and
technology.

- **Industry-specific museums,** particularly where the
methods and scale of production have undergone
radical change. Many of these museums are run by
the industries themselves. Some are working
museums. Not all are well advertised. If a particular
industry interests you and your pupils, try contacting
the Public Relations Division of the major firms in that
industry in order to find out what resources and what
visits (or visitors to you) are available.

- **War museums.** These are replete with examples of
rapid technological advance, not only in armaments
and war machines but also in areas such as food
technology, clothing, communications.

- **Transport museums,** many of which are working
museums.

- **Special events,** such as Steam Fayres, featuring, for
example, yesteryear steam-powered road vehicles
and agricultural machinery, old tools, vintage cars,
fairground rides, fairground organs, etc.

- **Open days** operated by preservation societies.

- The programme **Water Works** includes scenes at
**Eureka! The Museum for Children,** Discovery Rd,
Halifax, West Yorkshire, HX1 2NE, Information Line
01426 983191. The museum offers hands-on
experience for children up to the age of 12, including
those with special needs and wheelchair users.

- The programme **Park and Ride** includes scenes
at **Satrosphere,** run by SATRO (Science and
Technology Regional Organisation), where there is
hands-on experience. To locate your nearest SATRO,
phone SCSST on 0171 294 2431. If you are looking
for in-service training opportunities in science and
technology, phone SCSST.

- There is a **National Telephone Kiosk Collection**
within the **Avoncroft Museum of Historic Buildings,**
Stoke Heath, Bromsgrove, Worcestershire B60 4JR,
Tel 01527 831886. Kiosks on view date back over 70
years. Some of them work and can be tried out.
Collectively, they offer an intriguing study of change
and development in design. The buildings at the
Avoncroft Museum of Historic Buildings cover more
than 600 years of building, from medieval half
timber-framed to a 1940s pre-fab. In Bath, there are
fascinating postboxes and a postal museum. Tel
01225 460333